DIARY
OF A
VILLAGER
BUTCHER

BOOKS KID

TABLE OF CONTENTS

Day 1

Close your eyes and take a deep breath.

Smell that? That's the aroma of Butcher's Family Meat and it's the best smell in the world.

My name's Brutus and I'm the latest in a long line of butchers serving our village with the best tasting meat in all Minecraftia.

People come from far and wide to sample my sumptuous, melt-in-the-mouth meat, marinated in my special secret sauce. It's a recipe that's been passed down from father to son through the generations. Many people have offered us a fortune to tell them the unique combination of herbs and spices we use to make the meat taste so good, but we'll never sell out. Our family reputation is far too important to give up just for money.

"Morning, Brutus. Some of your finest pork chops, please!"

I looked up to see Troy, the village leader walking into the shop.

"Of course," I beamed, turning to select the best cuts for Troy. I always make sure that I set aside some meat for him. Not only is he a regular customer and I like to look after my regulars, as the village leader, he has the power to make or break my business. He rules the village with a rod of iron. If the traders don't maintain the highest of standards, he makes us give our shop to someone else. Only last month, Jasper the tool smith was forced to pack up his things and leave town. Marshall, the new tool smith, has been working extra hard to prove to Troy that he deserves a shop.

It's a lot of pressure – or it would be if I didn't know that my family secret recipe means that my meat will always taste delicious, even if it's cooked by the worst cook in the world.

"There you go," I said, handing Troy a bag filled with pork chops. "I've added an extra piece of bacon for you as a special treat."

"Thank you, Brutus." Troy took the bag from me. "That's what I always appreciate when I come in here. Your great customer service."

I breathed a sigh of relief as he left the shop. Even though I knew that I didn't have to worry about losing my business, it was always stressful dealing with Troy. You never knew what kind of mood he would be in and an angry Troy was never fun.

Day 2

"Good morning, Brutus."

I looked up to see Troy coming into the shop.

"Hello, Troy," I replied. "Two days in a row! That's unusual for you. To what do I owe this pleasure?"

"As you may know, the annual village summer barbecue is coming up," Troy told me. "This year, I've invited some very special guests, dignitaries from all the surrounding villages. I want them to see that we have the best village in all Minecraftia, so we're going to decorate the village and really put on a show. I want all the other village leaders to go away feeling jealous that their village isn't anywhere near as good as mine."

Privately, I thought that it wasn't just his village. It belonged to all of us villagers. Still, I didn't want to say anything to annoy him. We all knew that Troy had a temper.

"Anyway," Troy went on. "Obviously, we want to make sure that they're all well fed, which is where you come in. I want you to provide all the meat, all marinated in your special sauce so we can show the other leaders what they're missing. People are still talking about the incredible barbecue your father catered all those years ago and I want to put on a meal that is so amazing, people will never forget it."

I raised my eyebrows. It was a big request. Dad's barbecues were legendary and even with the family recipe, he was an incredible butcher for me to live up to. It was a big challenge.

"I'll certainly do my best," I promised.

"You need to do more than your best," warned Troy. "You need to give me the best barbecue Minecraftia has ever seen. If you don't, then you don't deserve the title of villager butcher and I'll be forced to give your shop to someone else, which will be the end of your family in this town. Do you want to be responsible for your family being forced to leave the village?"

I gulped. "No."

"Then give me what I want."

Troy turned and stomped out of the shop, leaving me wondering what I could do to make the family recipe taste even better than it already did.

Day 3

After Troy had made it clear that he expected me to provide food that was out of this world for the barbecue, I'd spent all night worrying how I was going to impress him and the other leaders. At last, I'd come up with an idea to experiment with the proportions of herbs and spices, adding in a new ingredient or two, to give people a choice of flavors.

The real secret was the amount of time the meat was left to marinade. Don't tell anyone I told you, will you?

Shutting up the shop early, I walked through the village, waving hello and greeting all the villagers rushing around, decorating the village in preparation for the barbecue. Clearly, Troy had gone around threatening everyone to do their best, just as he had me. Whatever you might think of his methods, they certainly worked.

Much as I would have loved to stop and chat with my friends, I was a butcher on a mission. I needed to go and prepare my meat so that even Troy would be stunned at how good it was.

I hurried out of the village and into the forest. Nobody knew, but I had a secret store out there where I kept my meat and prepared it for sale. It was the only way that I could guarantee myself privacy and know that nobody was spying on me to try and steal my recipe. I did a lot of experimentation out there, coming up with new ways of preparing meat, although so far, I had yet to find something as good as my family's traditional recipe.

That was all going to change. When I returned to the village, I'd be taking with me the best meat anyone had ever tasted.

Day 4

At last, I reached my shelter, the place where I stored all my meat while preparing it for sale. Here I was safe from prying eyes and I could work undisturbed to make sure that Troy had the quality he was looking for.

"What are you doing?"

I jumped and whirled round. Standing in front of me was a child. I didn't recognize him from the village, but if I was honest, I didn't really pay much attention to the village children. They all looked the same to me.

"What are *you* doing?" I countered.

"You looked interesting," he said. "I wanted to see what you were going to do. My parents are busy decorating the village and I was bored, so when I noticed you leaving the village, I decided to follow you and have some fun. So what are you doing?"

"None of your business," I snapped.

"Don't be like that," pleaded the child. "My name is Doug. What's yours?"

"None of your business," I repeated firmly.

"Come on, mister. Why are you being like this? Is it because you're trying to keep something secret? Don't worry. I'm really good at keeping secrets. I won't tell anyone what you've got in there, I promise. What is it? A zombie? A skeleton?"

He crowded up against the window, trying to get a glimpse of what was inside.

"Get away from there!" I ordered.

"I can't see anything," pouted Doug. "There are only shelves piled high with meat. Are you keeping a pet?"

He'd seen my meat! What was I going to do? If he went back to the village and told people what he'd seen, then I'd have other butchers coming out here, trying to steal my secret formula.

I did the only thing I could think of.

"All right," I sighed. "If you promise not to tell anyone what you see in here, you can come in."

Opening the door to my shelter, for the first time ever, someone who wasn't a member of my family came into my hidden meat storage hut.

Day 5

"Do you ever cut the meat like this? Is it better to make the chop thin or thick? Am I supposed to season on one side or two?"

I sighed and rolled my eyes at the never ending questions. I was already regretting letting Doug into my private workshop. The child never stopped talking! It was almost as though he didn't care whether I answered or not. He was just enjoying the sound of his own voice.

"Have you got those chops ready?" I asked, setting aside one set of marinades. As much as I believed Doug when he said that he wasn't going to tell anyone about my shelter, that didn't mean that I was going to trust him with mixing up the sauce. Cutting the meat was as much responsibility as he was going to get.

"Yes, sir!" Doug passed over the chops he'd been working on. Holding them up to inspect them, I was pleasantly surprised.

"Impressive," I nodded. "You've managed to get a consistent cut so that all the chops are the same size. I must admit that I wasn't expecting you to be able to do that. I thought I was going to have redo all your work."

"I'm a quick student," beamed Doug. "I've always wanted to be a butcher, so when I saw you leaving the village by yourself, I figured that this was the perfect opportunity to get you on my own so that I could learn from the best. Everyone knows that you're the greatest butcher in Minecraftia."

"Thank you, Doug. But don't think that a few compliments are going to persuade me to give you my secret recipe. That's strictly for family members only."

"I understand."

Doug bent his head over his work so that I wouldn't see the solitary tear trickling down his cheek, but I noticed it anyway. I felt bad for upsetting the boy, but for all I knew, he could be a member of one of the rival butchery families. I was never going to tell him how I got the meat to taste so good.

Day 6

I placed the final strips of meat in the sauce and put them up on a shelf to marinate.

"Right," I said to Doug. "We've done all we can do for now. We need to leave the meat to soak up the flavors and that takes time. Shall we take a walk in the forest while we're waiting?"

"Sure," smiled Doug.

I locked up the shelter, making sure that my meat was safe while the marinade worked its magic.

"Where are we going?" asked Doug, trotting along next to me.

"To my shelter by the lake," I replied.

"Shelter by the lake? Wow." Doug's eyes widened. "You have a *lot* of shelters!"

"I do," I nodded. "Most of the villagers are too afraid to come into the forest because they might meet a monster.

That means that I've been able to build shelters in the best places, since nobody else wants to come out here. I have my meat preparation shelter and then I have my shelter by the lake, which is where I go to relax while the food is marinating. The views are incredible."

"It sounds awesome. I can't wait to see it!"

Doug started to skip off down the path ahead of me, leaving me to amble along behind, enjoying the quiet. For once, Doug wasn't talking nonstop because he was so excited about exploring the forest.

"Look at this, Brutus!"

Doug was standing at the edge of a clearing and I rushed forward to see what Doug was pointing at. As I reached his side, I couldn't believe what I saw.

"Look at all this meat!" exclaimed Doug, running forward to gather it up. "You could add your special sauce and sell it!"

"No, Doug! Put it down, right now!" I batted a steak out of his hands.

"Why?" Doug pouted, looking forlornly at the meat on the floor.

"Because that meat's rotten" I explained. "There's clearly been a zombie battle here, which isn't good. There haven't been any zombies around here for a while. I'd hate to think that they were coming back."

"But couldn't you do something with the meat anyway?" asked Doug. "You're such a good butcher that you could make anything taste great."

"It's kind of you to say so," I chuckled, "but even if it did taste good, it wouldn't change the fact that the meat's rotten. I couldn't feed that to anyone. If they got sick because of my meat, Troy would throw me out of the village faster than you can say "zombie bait!""

"Do you think there are any zombies around?" Doug edged towards me nervously.

"It's all right. You're perfectly safe during the day," I reassured him. "Zombies burst into flame in the sunshine. Anyway, with any luck, they've all been defeated in this battle, although I can't imagine who could have done that. The villagers are terrible at fighting and none of them come out here…"

"Because of the zombies," finished Doug.

"Exactly. We'd better hurry. There's still a few hours left in the day, but once the sun goes down, any remaining zombies will head straight for us. We'll be safe in my shelter for the night."

Although I knew that zombies couldn't come out during the day, I didn't want to risk being wrong. The sooner we got to the shelter, the safer we would be.

Day 7

"GROAN!"

I was woken by the sound of something moaning. I reached by my bed for the large stick I kept there to chase away zombies. It was the one problem with having a shelter in the forest. Sometimes, overzealous zombies tried to get in and I had to bang on the walls to scare them away.

"GROAN!"

The sound came again, and I realized that it wasn't coming from outside – it was *inside* the shelter. Had the zombies managed to break through the door?

Heart pounding, I made my way towards the front room.

"GROAN!"

"Doug!"

I rushed to where the child was lying across the couch, moaning and clutching his stomach.

"My tummy," he complained. "It hurts!"

Feeling his forehead, he was slightly feverish and he wasn't looking well at all.

"Oh Doug," I sighed. "You didn't eat the rotten meat, did you?"

Doug nodded miserably. "I'm sorry, Brutus. I thought it would be all right. I'd been watching you closely while we were preparing the meat and I thought that I'd copied your recipe perfectly."

"I told you that it didn't matter what you did. That meat was rotten! Now you've got food poisoning."

"Food poisoning!" gasped Doug. "That sounds serious. Am I going to die?"

"No, no." I shook my head. "You haven't eaten enough meat for it to be fatal. But you're going to feel pretty rough for the rest of the day, so you'd better just stay where you are and I'll bring you some soup later when your tummy has settled down."

Doug fell back on the couch and within moments, he was fast asleep. Poor thing. It had been unwise to eat the rotten meat, but I knew from personal experience how horrible it was to have food poisoning and he was only young.

With any luck, he'd be feeling better after a good sleep. The last thing I wanted was a sick child stuck in my shelter for days. I'd been babysitting for long enough already.

Day 8

"Are you feeling better today?" I asked Doug.

"Yes, thank you," he replied, helping himself to some bacon for breakfast.

"Great! I can take you home then," I beamed.

"I said I'm feeling better, not that I'm completely recovered," Doug corrected. "I'm not ready to go home just yet. If I tried to walk back to the village, I think I'd faint from exhaustion! No, I think we should stay here and go fishing. Relaxing by the water is the best thing I could do right now."

"Fishing?" My heart sank. My shelter was by the lake because of the view, not because there were lots of fish about. I left catching them to the fishermen upriver. I was terrible at fishing!

"Yes. Come on – it'll be fun!"

"But I'm a butcher," I protested. "I don't know anything about fishing."

"It's okay. I'll teach you," promised Doug. "It's very easy. You'll see."

"All right then," I huffed. "If you're sure that you're not well enough to go home, we'll stay here and fish for a while."

"Awesome!" Doug jumped down from the kitchen table and rushed off to gather together equipment, looking remarkably lively for a child who was supposed to be too ill to go home.

We spent the day fishing and despite Doug's reassurance that fishing was easy, I didn't manage to catch a single fish. It seemed as though every time I threw my line in, the fish ran away, laughing at me.

Doug had better luck than I did. After pulling out a pair of leather boots and a fishing rod that looked uncannily like one I'd lost in the lake a few months ago, he managed to get a couple of fish.

"Fish for dinner!" he crowed.

"If you insist," I muttered, although I didn't see what was so great about fish. Give me a nice chop any day of the week!

Day 9

"Did you have fun fishing yesterday?" I asked Doug, as we locked up my shelter to go out into the forest.

"Oh, yes! We should do it again. Can we fish today too?"

"I'm sorry." I shook my head. "I need to get back to my meat. It should have been marinating for long enough now, so I need to start transporting it back to the village. You can help me if you like."

"All right," sighed Doug, pouting and hanging his head. Scuffing his foot along the floor, a slow, wicked grin spread across his face. "Tag! You're it!"

He tapped me on the back and ran off through the trees.

"Doug! Come back!" I called. "You'll get lost and eaten by zombies!"

"You'd better catch me, then!" he yelled back.

"All right. But I warn you. I run fast!"

I chased after Doug, but when I found him, he had a stick in his hand.

"This is my sword," he announced. "On guard, monster!"

"Monster, am I? We'll see about that."

Grabbing the nearest stick, I started towards Doug, beginning a fast and furious sword fight. That kid is going to be an excellent fighter when he grows up!

When he jabbed at my stomach, I grabbed the stick, pretending he'd impaled me.

"Argh!" I groaned. "You got me!"

Falling back, I lay still on the ground. "I'm dead," I whispered. "You can tell I'm dead because my tongue's sticking out!"

Laughing, Doug started tickling me under the arms.

"You're not dead!" he giggled. "Unless you're a zombie and zombies can't laugh!"

"You got me. I'm not dead. I'm a tickle monster!"

Roaring, I sat up and started tickling Doug.

We had so much fun together that I completely lost track of time. By the time I noticed the sun going down over the horizon, it was far too late for us to make it back to my meat store.

We were going to have to spend another night by the lake.

Day 10

"I had so much fun with you in the forest yesterday," Doug told me. "Can we do it again?"

"I'm sorry, Doug," I replied. "We've spent far too long out here. I really need to get back to my meat. We can always come out to the forest some other day, but with the barbecue coming, I have to make sure that everything is back at the village in plenty of time. I don't want to make Troy angry if there isn't enough food for everyone."

"Oh come on, Brutus. Is one more day really going to make that much difference?"

"Yes, it really is," I said firmly. "If my meat marinates for too long, it will taste all wrong. I've spent as much time with you as I possibly can, but now it's time to go back to the village. Now come on. We need to get moving."

"I'm not going!" Doug stuck his tongue out at me and ran off.

"Come back!" I called, rushing after him. "There are zombies in these woods. It's not safe for you to be out here alone!"

"I'm coming back if you can catch me!" came the reply.

I ran as fast as I could, but Doug was surprisingly speedy for such a little kid and I soon lost sight of him among the trees.

"Stop being silly!" I yelled. "We need to go back to the village, right now."

"Make me!"

I whirled round, but I couldn't see where the voice had come from.

"Get out here right now, or... or..."

"Or what?"

I tried desperately to think of a good threat, but nothing came to mind.

"Or you won't have any meat at the barbecue," I finally finished.

"You can't stop me!" taunted Doug. "I'll tell Troy about you."

"Tell Troy!" I gasped. "You wouldn't!"

"Oh yes, I would!"

There was nothing for me to do but try and find Doug. I looked everywhere for him, his giggles when I hunted in the wrong place driving me nuts.

At last I found him crouched in a little hollow under a tree. "Got you!" I cried. "Now you need to keep your end of the bargain. We're going back to my meat store and I don't want any more arguments from you."

"Aren't you forgetting something?" Doug pointed at the horizon. "The sun is about to go down and there are zombies in this forest, remember?"

"Oh yes." My shoulders slumped. We were going to have to spend yet another night by the lake when I should be back at the village by now. "All right. We'll stay here until the sun comes up, but first thing in the morning, we're going back to my meat store and if you run away, this time I'll leave you for the zombies to munch on."

"Don't worry. I'll come back to your meat store tomorrow," promised Doug.

Day 11

True to his word, Doug was ready to hit the road as soon as the first ray of light shone through the shelter window.

"Come on, slowpoke. What's taking you so long?" he teased, as I made sure that my shelter was properly locked up.

"You can never be too careful," I warned. "Even out here in the middle of the forest. I'm not going to leave my shelter open for zombies to move in."

We hurried along down the path towards my meat store. We should have returned three days ago, so I hoped that Troy wouldn't be too angry with me for the delay.

At last, we could see my meat shelter up ahead. The sight gave me an extra boost of energy and I practically ran towards it.

When I reached the door, my blood ran cold. Someone had been here and kicked it in.

"Nooo!" I screamed, running inside.

Empty. It was completely empty.

Every single shelf had been cleared of my carefully marinating meat.

"Oh no!" Doug came to stand next to me. "You've been robbed. Who could have done such a thing?"

"You!" I span around, so mad that I was practically spitting. "This is your fault!"

"How is it my fault?" Doug's bottom lip quivered as he fought back tears. "I'm your friend!"

"My friend? Pah!" I wanted to scream, shout, throw things around, I was so angry. "You're not my friend. You deliberately kept me away from my shelter so that your fellow thieves could clear out my secret stash. All that time we were playing games, you knew that there were people back here clearing out my secret stash."

"I didn't!" protested Doug.

"No more! No more of your lies! Get out of here before I say something I regret!"

"I didn't do anything!" wailed Doug, but he could see from my face that I meant what I was saying and he ran off down the path in the direction of the village.

I couldn't believe it. All my hard work gone, thanks to that kid. Well, that was the last time I was going to let anyone help me out around here. I should have known that it was a bad idea. There's a reason why we keep our family recipe in the family. Nobody else can be trusted.

Day 12

"Here piggy, piggy, piggy!"

I walked through the trees, calling out to the animals that lived in the forest. I had a lot of meat to replace and not much time to replace it in.

Luckily for me, the animals around here are stupid and slow moving, so it didn't take long before I started to build up a good replacement supply, but I was still going to have to do all the preparation from scratch.

It took a lot of trips out into the forest to find pigs and cows, but by the end of the day, my shelves were piled with meat once more.

It was work that I could have done without, though. I should have been back at the village by now, Troy heaping praise on me for my delicious meat. If I ever saw Doug again, he would get the telling off of a lifetime!

Day 13

Sprinkling over my secret blend of herbs and spices, I hoped that the changes I'd made to the recipe would make up for the fact that I wasn't going to be able to leave the meat marinating for as long as I should. Since Doug had delayed me for so long, time was short and I needed to be back for the barbecue before Troy lost his temper with me.

At last, the final few chops were steeped in marinade and I curled up in the middle of the shelter to watch over them. It wasn't as comfortable as my shelter by the lake, but I didn't care. I wasn't going to let the meat out of my sight until I'd personally handed it over to Troy.

As I drifted off to sleep, the sounds of zombies crashing through the trees filtered through the shelter walls. I'd had enough of being out in the forest. The sooner I was back in the safety of the village, the better.

Day 14

I carefully wrapped the meat up before stuffing it into my backpacks. By the time I was done, the bags were bulging and my back ached within moments of slinging the backpacks over my shoulders, but at least I knew that the village was going to have enough meat for the barbecue.

As I headed up the road towards home, I couldn't help but smile at the sight of my village. While I'd been away, the villagers had worked hard to decorate it in preparation for the barbecue and the place was transformed. It looked incredible, with all the houses redecorated in bright, festive colors to celebrate the summer.

Walking into the village, I saw my dad coming towards me.

"Brutus!" he beamed. "I'm so glad to see you back. We were starting to get a little worried that this was going to be a barbecue without meat, so I would have to come out of retirement, just this once."

"You know me, dad," I smiled. "I never let a party down! I've got all the meat right here in these backpacks. I just need to give them to Troy and I can help out with the other barbecue preparations."

"I think Troy is busy right now," dad told me. "Best not to disturb him – he's had a bad day. Apparently, he's just heard that one of the other village leaders threw a party recently and he wasn't invited. Now he's all worried that our barbecue won't be as good and he's shouting at anyone who even looks in his general direction. Leave the meat out at the back of the grill for the time being. I'll let him know that you've dropped it off."

"Thanks dad." Truth be told, I was glad for the excuse not to have to see Troy. I didn't want to have to explain to him why it had taken me so long to deliver the meat.

"Anyway, while you're here, there's someone I want you to meet," dad said.

"Really? Who?"

"Your cousin. His family have come to the village to help out with the barbecue and I just know that the two of you are going to get along. He's over there. Come on. Let me introduce you."

I followed dad as he walked over to the other side of the village square.

"Here he is. Your cousin Doug!"

I gasped as the kid who'd followed me out to my shelter ran over to give me a big hug.

"Brutus!" he cried. "It's so good to see you!"

"Oh?" Dad looked puzzled. "You two know each other?"

"We've met," I said through clenched teeth.

"Then I guess you two have got a lot to catch up about. You took a really long time going to fetch that meat, you know."

"Yeah. You already said that, dad," I muttered as my dad strode off to make sure the meat was safely stored.

"So. What do you do around the village for fun?" asked Doug.

I shook my head and sighed. This was going to be the worst barbecue ever.

Day 15

"Is this your store? It's so cool!"

It took all my self-control not to bite Doug's head off, as he browsed my butcher's store. Just because he was family didn't mean that I didn't still suspect him of having something to do with the theft. Maybe his parents wanted to move into my village and take over. Anything was possible.

"Oh come on, Brutus. You can't still be mad with me. You're not still mad with me, are you?"

"Of course I am," I snapped. "I know you had something to do with the theft of my meat. Don't deny it!"

"It wasn't anything to do with me, I swear!" protested Doug. "I was as shocked by the theft as you were."

"Oh really? Then why did you go out of your way to stop me coming back from the lake? The only explanation is that you were making sure your fellow thieves had enough time to take everything."

"That's not true," countered Doug. "The reason I was trying to get you to stay with me is because I think you're awesome. Everyone always says what a great butcher you are and I wanted to learn from you. I figured that if you knew that we were cousins, you'd have to be nice to me because we're related. I wanted to spend time with you without you knowing who I was so that I'd see what you're really like."

I gulped. Doug was right. I would have been nicer to him if I'd known that he was my cousin. I wasn't going to risk dad telling me off. Instead, I'd been grumpy and short with him. Dad was not going to be happy.

"And do you know what?" he continued.

"What?"

"I had the best time ever!" Doug beamed. "I had so much fun with you. We played so many great games and even though you didn't trust me with your recipe, I learned a lot from you about how to prepare meat."

"I'm glad you enjoyed yourself," I said gruffly, still not sure whether to believe what he was saying or if he was still part of some plot to get me into trouble.

"Anyway," he went on. "I've been looking for clues and I have a few ideas about who might have stolen your meat."

"Is that right?"

"It is," Doug nodded eagerly. "And if we find your meat, we can bring it back before the barbecue. I know that you were disappointed you weren't able to let the new batch marinate for longer, so wouldn't it be cool if we could bring back the stolen meat?"

"It would," I agreed.

Doug was annoying and irritating, but he had a point. I'd be so much happier if I was able to recover my stolen meat and bring it back for the party. After all, you can never have enough meat at a barbecue!

Day 16

"Are you up for an adventure?" asked Doug.

"Not really," I replied. After all, the last time Doug and I hung out together, it ended with all my meat being stolen.

"That's a shame. I don't see how you're going to get your meat back without one…" He smiled slyly, turning away, although I could see him looking at me out of the corner of his eyes.

"All right," I sighed. "What kind of an adventure?"

"Well, do you remember when I said that I had an idea for who might have taken the meat?"

"Yes."

"Well, as I was coming into the village, I saw what looked like an adventurer's camp not far from the main access road. I think the stolen meat might be there."

"What makes you think that?"

"For a start, they had a campfire going and I could smell the meat they were cooking."

"So? All that means is that they already had their own meat. Why would they need to steal mine?"

"Maybe they ran out?" Doug suggested. "Maybe they heard about how good your meat tastes and they couldn't afford to trade for it? There are lots of reasons why people steal things in Minecraftia."

"I'm still not convinced that that is enough evidence to prove that they are the thieves. What else makes you think they're responsible?"

"They haven't come into the village yet," Doug said. "As we were traveling, we came across lots of people staying in the forest, but they've all arrived in the village for the barbecue. I haven't seen anyone around town who looks like the people who were camping. Surely that must mean that they're up to no good?"

"Perhaps," I nodded slowly. "It could also mean that they were going somewhere completely different. Not everyone has been invited to the barbecue."

"But it's got to be worth checking out, hasn't it?" asked Doug. "Come on, Brutus. The camp wasn't all that far away and you've already delivered your meat. They don't really need you around here – they've got plenty of people making the village ready for the party. You can sneak out and check on the camp. If I'm wrong, then at least you've had a couple of days with me, so you won't have completely wasted your time."

I wasn't entirely convinced that I really wanted to spend any more time with Doug, but if there was a chance I might be able to recover my meat, it was worth the risk.

"All right," I said at last. "We'll go and take a look at this camp of yours."

"Yes!" Doug leaped up, punching the air with his fist. I don't think I'd ever seen anyone so excited at spending time with me. It was a most peculiar feeling.

Day 17

"There's the camp," Doug whispered as we lay on our bellies, crouching down so they wouldn't see us spying on them from up the hill. "I was right – they haven't come to the village."

"Humph," I grunted. Just because they hadn't come to the village didn't mean that they were up to no good, but at the same time, it was suspicious that they were still out here and hadn't moved on.

"We're going to need to get a closer look," decided Doug, scrambling down the hill before I could tell him to stop. He left me with no choice but to follow after him, but he was surprisingly fast for such a little fellow and he'd run all the way to a tree next to the camp before I was able to catch up with him. He was lucky nobody saw him.

"Shh!" Doug put a finger up to his lips to warn me to be quiet, but I didn't need to be told. I could see the sharp blades strapped to the belts of the adventurers. I was no good in a fight and I had no desire to be caught spying.

Doug nudged me with his elbow, pointing over to an enclosure at the back of the encampment. I had to stifle a cry when I spotted what he'd seen.

Wolves! Countless wolves roaming around in their pen while an adventurer leaned over and threw meat at them.

Not just any meat, either. *My* meat.

I'd seen enough. Tapping Doug on the shoulder, I motioned with my head that it was time for us to leave before we were discovered.

"Can you believe it?" gasped Doug when we were out of earshot. "They're using your meat to train wolves."

"Not just any wolves, either. I think they're training them up to be an attack force. I think they're going to invade the village," I said grimly.

"We have to get back!" exclaimed Doug. "We need to warn the others. If those adventurers attack the village while all the village leaders are there, they won't just have your village under their control. They'll have conquered the whole area!"

"That's not going to happen," I told him. "Not on my watch. Come on. Let's go and tell Troy what we've seen. A few iron golems should be enough to see them off before things get nasty."

Day 18

I'd never run as fast for so long in all my life. By the time we reached the village, I was out of breath and felt as though I was going to have a heart attack. Once we'd dealt with the invaders, I was definitely going to start jogging to get my fitness levels back up.

"Troy's over there." Doug tugged on my arm and pointed to where the village leader was criticizing a banner one of the villagers was making.

"Village has *two* Ls, you idiot!" he scolded. "You're going to have to paint the whole thing again."

"Troy! Troy! I'm so glad I've found you!" I rushed over to Troy, panting to catch my breath and get the words out.

"Yes? What is it? Can't you see that I'm busy?" snapped the village leader.

"There's an attack!" I panted. "I mean, there's going to be an attack. Outside the village. There are people!"

"Of course there are people," Troy sneered. "They're gathering for the barbecue."

"Not these people," I warned. "They're staying outside of the village, training wolves to slaughter us in our sleep!"

"Don't be ridiculous. They'll have the wolves for protection. It can be dangerous out there in the forest. There are zombies lurking behind every tree."

"Not these wolves." I shook my head, frustrated that Troy refused to believe me. "They're going to attack us with them. We won't stand a chance, not even with our iron golems. We have to go and attack them now while they're not expecting it or this village and all the others in the area will be defeated!"

"Stop being so hysterical!" Troy ordered. "The Minecraftians in that camp are here for the barbecue, nothing more, nothing less."

"But they haven't even been invited!"

"It doesn't matter. Everyone is welcome. This is going to be the most amazing barbecue in the history of barbecues and the more people who are here to enjoy it, the better. This is going to be one of those events that everyone will be talking about for years to come."

"But Troy-"

"Enough!" he barked. "I'm not hearing any more from you about this supposed attack. You're being silly and if you say anything to upset the guests with stories about an army of wolves, then I'll get the iron golems to throw you in prison and toss away the key."

I knew when I was wasting my breath and Troy wasn't joking about prison. He'd once put a villager in jail just for feeding the chickens when Troy had decided that chickens were banned from the town square.

"Sorry to bother you," I muttered. I desperately wanted to try and convince Troy to change his mind, but I knew when I was beaten. I just had to hope that he was right and I was wrong, because if those wolves attacked the village, we were doomed.

Day 19

"Brutus! I've been looking for you everywhere."

I looked up to see Troy making his way towards me. At first, I thought he'd changed his mind about the attack and was coming to tell me to lead the charge on the camp, but then I saw the dark look on his face.

"What is it, Troy? What's wrong?"

"That meat you brought."

"What about it?"

"It's terrible! I arranged a little pre-barbecue taster and everyone hated it!"

My heart sank. The last minute marinade I'd made clearly wasn't as good as I'd hoped.

"I'm so sorry, Troy. Perhaps if you leave the meat to marinade for longer?"

"Marinade? For longer?" Troy looked like his head was about to explode. "What do I look like? A butcher?"

"Er…" There was nothing wrong with being a butcher, so I wasn't sure why Troy was so annoyed at the thought.

"Meat preparation is your job, not mine. I've got far more important things to worry about. I look to you to make sure that everyone has enough to eat at the barbecue and they love every single bite. I don't want people to get food poisoning because you're too lazy to do your job."

"I wasn't too lazy!" I protested. "My meat was stolen!"

"What? By the people who are supposedly planning an attack on the village?" said Troy sarcastically. "I thought I warned you against making up stories like that."

"They're not… I mean, it isn't… I wasn't…"

It was no good. I couldn't think of anything to say that wouldn't make Troy angrier, so in the end, I decided to say nothing at all.

"If you keep this up, I'm going to take your store away," Troy warned. "If I find out that anyone has left the barbecue because of your tall tales, just one person, that's it. Not only will I take away your store and give it to someone who can supply me with better quality meat, I'll banish you from the village forever!"

"Forever!" I gasped.

"This is your final warning. Get yourself together or get out of my village."

Troy turned and stomped off, leaving me stunned.

Day 20

"Doug! Just the kid I was looking for."

I found Doug playing with some of the other villager children.

"Hey, Brutus. How are you doing?"

"Come over here and I'll tell you."

Taking Doug by the elbow, I pulled him away from the other children so no one could overhear us. After Troy's warning, I wasn't going to risk anyone hearing what I was about to say.

"Remember when you asked me if I wanted to go on an adventure?" I began.

"Yes."

"Well I do. I want to go on the kind of adventure that you only read about in books. I want to save the village and be a big hero. In short, I want to go back to that camp, get my meat and stop the attack on the village. What's more, I want to do it with you by my side."

"Really?" The look of delight that spread over Doug's face warmed my heart. I had no idea how important to him it was for the two of us to spend time together.

"Yes, really," I laughed. "But there's one condition."

"What's that?"

"You can't tell anyone."

"But what about mom and dad? I got into so much trouble when I spent those days with you by the lake. If I disappeared off again, they'd ground me for life."

"Hmmm." I thought for a moment. "How about this? We tell them that I need to prepare more meat because the last batch tasted bad, which is true. They will think that we've gone back to my secret shelter when in reality, we'll be going back to the camp. They'll only find out what actually happened when we come back victorious."

"I love it!" cried Doug. "If they know that I'm with you, then they won't mind what we do. They told me that I should try and learn as much as I can from you while we're here, so if they think that I'm studying butchery for a few days, they'll be really happy. They'll probably give us snacks and supplies for the journey to your shelter!"

"Then it's settled. Let's go and find your parents now and tell them where we're going. The sooner we leave, the sooner we can save the village."

"Hurray!" Doug cheered. His enthusiasm was infectious and I found myself cheering with him. We were going to save the village, just the two of us.

Day 21

There was something deliciously naughty about sneaking away from the village in the opposite direction to my shelter. Doug's parents had given him permission to come away with me for a few days, but only if he behaved himself and did everything I told him to.

Funnily enough, the prospect of disobeying his parents had made him so excited that he'd behaved perfectly so far. I hoped that this continued – there was no doubt that we were embarking upon an extremely dangerous mission and if he decided to run away by himself again, I might not be able to protect from the dangers lurking in the woods.

Speaking of which, the sun was starting to set and we needed to find somewhere safe to spend the night.

"Can't we just build a shelter?" asked Doug, as I started poking around the trees and bushes, looking for a hole we could hide in.

"We could," I replied. "But I didn't bring an axe with me and do you fancy pulling down trees with your bare hands?"

"I suppose not," shrugged Doug, going over to have a look under another bush to see if it was a good place to hide.

GROAN!

"Zombies!" screamed Doug, leaping away from the bush. Sure enough, a pair of zombies lurched out from between the leaves. They must have been using the bush to shelter from the sun, but now it was dark enough for them to come out to look for food and we were on the menu!

"Quick! Over here!"

I beckoned to Doug and he scampered away from the zombies. Luckily, they were slow moving and we were able to outpace them, but I knew just how good a zombie's sense of smell was. I couldn't take the chance of resting and the zombies catching up to us, so I urged Doug to keep moving long past the point when his little legs just wanted to collapse.

"Here. I'll carry you."

I lifted Doug onto my shoulders and carried on plodding through the forest. It was now pitch black, every shadow seeming to hide a zombie. Whenever I heard a twig snap, I jumped, thinking it was a zombie reaching out to pull Doug from my shoulders.

I was so nervous and it was so dark that I didn't pay attention to where I was going. Suddenly, my foot slipped and we went tumbling down a hill. Down, down, down we fell, coming to land in a big pile of dirt at the bottom.

"Yuck!" splattered Doug, spitting dirt out. "That's disgusting!"

"Are you all right?" I asked anxiously, terrified that I'd hurt him when we fell down the hill.

"I'm OK. I just stink from whatever it is I've landed in," he complained.

"You stink?" That gave me an idea. "Right. Cover yourself with dirt from head to toe."

"Cover myself?" wailed Doug. "But I was trying to scrape it off. It smells disgusting!"

"Exactly!" I beamed, extremely proud of my clever idea. "The zombies won't be able to smell you and we can go to sleep under a bush without being bothered."

"I suppose so," sighed Doug, but he did as he was told, slapping on big handfuls of dirt until his whole body was covered. His parents would probably want to have words with me about the state of his clothes when we went back to the village, but at least their son wasn't going to end up as zombie bait.

"Come on. We can sleep under that bush over there."

I led Doug over to a thick bush surrounded by trees. We crawled underneath, covering ourselves with branches as best we could, before finally drifting off to sleep, too exhausted to keep our eyes open for zombies.

Day 22

I was woken up by the sun filtering through the leaves of the bush. We'd survived the night without any zombies finding us and now we needed to get to the camp to retrieve my meat.

"Wake up, Doug." I gently shook the sleeping child.

"What? Where are we?"

"We're out in the forest about to get my meat back, remember?"

"Oh yes. I was having the most amazing dream where I was living in a palace and wolves brought me meat for every meal. It was great!"

"Well maybe one day you'll sell enough meat to build your own palace, but for now, we need to think about how we're going to get my meat. The camp's not too far away now. If we're quick, we might be able to make it back to camp today before the sun sets."

Picking some apples to have for breakfast, we crept towards where we'd last seen the camp. As we drew near, the sound of wolf howls split the air and when we finally were close enough to spy on the adventurers, my heart sank. They'd managed to get more wolves, too many for the iron golems to fight alone. What was worse was that the men were in the middle of their fighting practice and even to my untrained eye, I could see that they were incredible.

We weren't going to stand a chance against them. Why wouldn't Troy listen to me?

We were doomed.

Day 23

I'd been too disheartened to go back to the village just yet, but after another night sleeping under the bush, I woke up with a resolve to do something, anything that might help the village. I might not be able to save them from the invaders, but I could at least make sure that they had a good meal before the attack.

Yes, I was going to get my meat back!

"What are you doing?" asked Doug sleepily, as I attempted to sneak out from under the bush without waking him.

Dang! I'd hoped to be able to get into the camp and back before he woke up.

"I'm going to go and fetch my meat."

"Great! I'll help you!"

Doug scrambled to his feet.

"No, you won't," I said firmly. "You're going to stay here where it's safe. I'll be back soon."

"But I could keep an eye out for you, warn you if anyone's coming."

"It's too dangerous." I shook my head.

"But Brutus, I want to help!"

"What did your parents tell you?" I said sternly.

"Do whatever you tell me to do," Doug muttered.

"Right. And I'm telling you to stay here until I get back. I'm going to try and sneak into their camp and get my meat. If I think it's too dangerous, I'll come straight back here and we can head back to the village without it. Troy might not believe me about the attack, but maybe we can find a few villagers who will or build a few traps to protect the village without Troy noticing. We'll do *something* and you can be a big part of it, I promise. But for now, I need you to stay here so I don't have to worry about you, OK?"

"OK," mumbled Doug.

I wasn't completely convinced he was going to wait here, but I didn't have any time to waste. It was still early and my plan was to get to the stores before the adventurers woke up.

Leaving Doug behind, I crept around the outskirts of the camp. I had a moment of panic when I went past the wolf enclosure, fearing they were going to howl a warning, but they were so tame that they simply sat and watched as I edged round their pen and towards where the meat was being stored.

Fortunately for me, the door wasn't locked, probably because the adventurers didn't think anyone would be foolish enough to try and steal from them. I knew that if they found me, they'd attack me on the spot to stop me warning the other villagers, little knowing that I'd already tried to warn them.

Holding my breath, I eased the door to the storage open and gasped when I saw what was inside.

My meat! My lovely meat! It was all there and it smelled delicious. While the adventurers might have stolen it to give to the wolves, they must have changed their minds once they realised how tasty it was. Well now, I was taking back what was rightfully mine.

There were a few backpacks hanging on hooks in the store. Quickly, I stuffed the meat into the bags. Carefully shutting the door, I tiptoed away, stifling the urge to cheer.

I'd done it! I'd saved my meat!

"Doug! Doug! I got my meat. We need to race back to the village."

Eagerly, I pushed my way underneath the bush, but there was no sign of the kid.

"Doug?"

"Help! Help! Somebody help me!"

The cry was distant, but unmistakeable. The adventurers had kidnapped Doug!

He had enough intelligence not to call me by name and give away the fact that I was nearby, but there was no way I was going to leave him in the hands of such wicked men. At the same time, I knew that I didn't stand a chance against their swords.

There was nothing else I could do. I turned and started running towards the village. Now that they'd taken Doug, Troy would *have* to believe me. If he sent an army out here, maybe we could still defeat the adventurers and catch them unawares.

Day 24

"Troy! Troy! You've got to help!"

As I ran into the village, I spotted the town leader talking to another villager.

"What is it now?" Troy huffed. "Can't you see that I'm busy choosing the right color tablecloth?"

"It's Doug. He's been kidnapped by the adventurers camping outside of the village."

"Don't be ridiculous," Troy chided. "There are no kidnappers in the area. This better not be an elaborate plan to try and trick me into believing that stupid story of yours about an attack."

"It's not a stupid story!" I protested.

"Enough!" snapped Troy. "I've warned you what will happen if you persist in this nonsense. Don't make me take away your store."

"Fine." Seeing Doug's parents across the town square, I raced over to them.

"Doug has been kidnapped!" I told them.

"Doug? Kidnapped?" His mom and dad started to laugh. This was not the reaction I'd been expecting.

"I'm sorry, Brutus," said Doug's dad. "I did tell Doug to behave himself while he was with you. He seemed to really like you, so I didn't think he would play any of his pranks. I'm afraid that Doug is just messing with you."

"He's not, I swear," I urged. "He really has been taken."

"No he hasn't," his mom replied. "He does this all the time. He's run away from you because he thinks it's funny. He'll be back when he's hungry so don't you worry. I'll make sure that he's punished for being naughty."

"Why won't any of you believe me?" I wailed, as Doug's parents walked away, chuckling at their son's apparent mischief. "Well, if none of you are going to help me, I guess I'm going to have to rescue him all by myself."

I wasn't going to leave Doug in the hands of those ruffians for a second longer than was necessary.

Day 25

"Good morning, Brutus. I don't often see you around my store. What brings you here on this fine day?"

Aaron the armor smith came over to me, a big smile on his face. I'd always liked Aaron and although I couldn't tell him the real reason why I wanted some armor, I knew that he'd be able to help me find the right armor for me.

"I'm looking for some armor," I told him.

"Is it a gift?" he asked. "It's a little unusual to give armor to another villager, but some people do like to give them as birthday presents, just in case."

"No, it's for me."

"For you?" Aaron raised an eyebrow and I blushed, wanting to tell him my plan, but too afraid of Troy to risk him discovering that I'd been telling people about the adventurers. "Not a problem. I'd recommend something light, like leather. If you're not used to armor, it can be very difficult to move around in it. You can always increase the amount of protection it offers by adding some enchantments at a small extra cost."

"Let's try some leather armor on then."

Aaron fetched some leather armor and started strapping it on my body. Oh my goodness, it weighed a ton!

"How can anyone do anything with this stuff on?" I complained. "I can barely move, let alone fight."

"To be fair, most adventurers are a little… stronger than you," said Aaron diplomatically.

"A little stronger? They'd have to be a LOT stronger to cope with this stuff! Get it off! It's hurting!"

Quickly, Aaron undid the buckles and pulled the armor off. I heaved a sigh of relief to be free of the burden.

"I've got some other armor you might like to try instead?" he offered. "It might be a little easier for you to move about in."

"I'm fine, thanks." I shook my head. I was wasting my time trying on armor when it was clear that it was going to slow me down far too much. I was just going to have to make sure that I dodged the adventurers' swords. I wouldn't need any armor if I wasn't hit in the first place, would I?

Day 26

"Hey there, Brutus. Long time, no see. What can I do for you today?"

Trevor the weapon smith grinned broadly when he saw me coming into his weapon store. He was one of the nicest people in town, always cheerful, always happy to help. It was strange to think that such a happy person was in the business of making weapons to kill monsters.

"I'd like a sword, please."

"A sword?" Trevor couldn't prevent a surprised look spreading over his face. "What do you want with one of those?"

I thought fast. It hadn't occurred to me that Trevor might ask questions about what I needed a sword for.

"I'm experimenting with new ways of getting meat," I finally replied. "I thought that maybe it might be a quicker way of getting bacon."

"I like your style," Trevor nodded. "Anything that brings more bacon into the world has got to be a good thing. All right, then. Let's find you a sword."

He brought out a lovely, shiny sword. "Here you go," he said. "A nice, light blade to get you started."

He handed it over to me, but as soon as he let go, the weight forced me to drop it.

"You said this was light!" I gasped.

"It is," shrugged Trevor. "But maybe the balance was wrong for you. Here, try this one."

It wasn't the balance. It didn't matter what sword I tried, they were all far too heavy for me to even lift, never mind use in a fight.

"It's no good," I complained, after the fifth sword I failed to pick up. "The swords are too much for me."

"Don't beat yourself up," consoled Trevor. "Swords aren't for everyone and at least you have other ways you can catch animals. You'll still be the town butcher for years to come, with or without a sword."

"Thanks, Trevor." I tried to sound happy about that, but of course, that hadn't been the reason why I needed a sword.

As it was, I couldn't wear armor and now I couldn't even wield a weapon. How was I going to be able to save Doug when I was so useless?

Day 27

I moped about town, depressed and at a loss for what to do. I was completely helpless and couldn't do anything to rescue Doug. I couldn't even get excited about the preparations for the barbecue, which was fast approaching. I was certain that the invaders would attack right in the middle of the party when everyone was distracted, so time was running out. I didn't like to think what could be happening to Doug right now.

"Do cheer up, Brutus," snapped Troy, bustling past me with his arms filled with party favors. "We're having a barbecue, not a funeral. One look at your face and you'll put people off their meat!"

The meat!

As Troy disappeared off in the direction of the town square, he didn't see the smile that spread over my face. Of course! Why didn't I think of it before? I was a butcher and what's the one thing butchers understand?

Meat!

My meat was the key to saving both Doug and the town. I had the perfect plan. The only question was whether I'd left it too late to put it into action.

Surreptitiously snatching up a few chops from the store room, I hurried out of the town. I was a butcher on a mission with no time to lose.

Day 28

If there were any zombies lurking in the forest, they probably took one look at my face and ran away as I raced towards the adventurers' camp. Nothing was going to stop me from saving Doug, not even a zombie.

As I drew near to the camp, I slowed, not wanting to be spotted by any guards that might be on duty. My plan relied on stealth and secrecy, no need for any armor or weaponry.

I ducked down behind a bush, dashing from one tree to another, as I concealed myself to get close to the camp. At one point, I froze, as two adventurers walked right past the tree where I was hiding, but they didn't spot me hiding so close to them and went on their way.

Eventually, I climbed a tree close to their camp where I could see everything that was going on without any of the adventurers spotting me. To my relief, Doug was tied up in the middle of the camp, seemingly unharmed. Whatever they were going to do to him, they hadn't done it yet and if I had anything to do with it, they never would.

I waited up in the tree until all the adventurers had gone to sleep. They seemed to be so smug that nobody was going to attack them that they didn't even bother posting any guards.

Good. That made it easier for me to teach them a lesson they were never going to forget.

Once I was certain that they were all asleep, I shimmied down the tree and snuck over to the wolves' enclosure.

"Here, wolfy, wolfy, wolfy," I whispered, waving a pork chop at the wolves.

Immediately, their ears pricked up as they sniffed the air in the direction of the chop. Carefully opening the gate to the enclosure so I wouldn't make any noise, wolves crowded around me, desperate to get to the meat, but too well trained to snatch it.

Like the Pied Piper of Hamlin, I held the chop high above my head as I lead the wolves through the forest and out towards my meat store. Although there wasn't much meat left after I'd delivered the latest batch for the barbecue, there was enough to attract the wolves.

"There you go, my little beauties," I murmured, as, one by one, the wolves dutifully trotted into the shelter. When the last one had gone in, I shut the door behind them, locking it so they couldn't go anywhere. I could hear the sound of happy wolves munching away on meat and I couldn't help but smile. I might not have destroyed the invading army –

yet – but the loss of their wolves would be a major blow to their forces and I hadn't finished with the adventurers.

Day 29

"Hey! Where have all the wolves gone? Fergus! Did you leave the enclosure open again? I warned you about that!"

I giggled to myself as I listened to the adventurers arguing between themselves when they discovered that their wolves had disappeared. I'd left the gate to the wolf pen open deliberately and it worked out just as I'd hoped. The adventurers were blaming each other for letting the wolves escape instead of looking for someone like me who'd set them free. They'd never guess that the wolves were safely locked up in my shelter on the other side of the forest and by the time I'd finished with them, wolves would be the last thing on their mind.

However, even without their wolves, the adventurers were fearsome fighters, so I needed to put the second part of my plan into action.

When Doug and I had disturbed the zombies in a bush, it gave me an idea. Now, I had a busy day ahead of me, as I rushed about the forest, finding where zombies were hidden and throwing blankets over them. Once they were protected from the sun, I then dragged them to a spot I'd picked out earlier so that they were all together in one, big, zombie army.

As the sun set over the horizon, I made sure that I was as far away from the zombies as possible, in case any of them woke early – and right next to the camp.

GROAN!

The sound of zombies waking from their sleep was my signal to act.

"Hey!" I yelled at the camp. "Idiots! You're here to attack my village, but I bet you can't even catch one villager!"

"Oh yeah?" came the answering cry. "Why should we even bother?"

That wasn't great. If the adventurers didn't chase after me, I wasn't going to be able to save Doug.

I thought fast. "Because if you don't catch me, how are you going to find out where your wolves are?"

"Our wolves?"

I knew that would get them moving!

I'd never ran as fast in all my life, but this was the most dangerous part of my plan and everything hinged on my ability to sprint.

"You can't catch me!" I called over my shoulder, as the adventurers ran after me. I felt one of them reach out to grab me, but it only gave me wings, spurring me on to run even faster.

At last, I spotted the zombie clearing up ahead and I ran through it, making as much noise as possible to get the zombies attention.

"Zombies!" I shouted. "It's an all you can eat buffet!"

"Zombies!" shouted the adventurers, but their cries were tinged with fear. I carried on running, but I could hear the sound of swords being drawn as the zombies turned on the adventurers.

Everything had worked out exactly as I hoped. I risked stopping for a moment to catch my breath and through the trees, I could see the adventurers fighting the zombies. Despite their strength, the adventurers were no match for the countless zombies I'd collected together. I had no idea there were so many living in the forest, and I never thought that I'd be so glad they were there, but as I watched, one by one, the adventurers fell in the face of the zombie might.

The invading attackers were defeated and I'd managed to do it without any help from Troy or the other villagers.

When I was certain that the zombies were going to finish off the adventurers, I headed back to the camp where poor old Doug was still tied up.

"Brutus!" he gasped when he saw me. "What are you doing? The adventurers are going to be back at any moment. Save yourself!"

"The adventurers aren't coming back any time soon," I told him, explaining what had happened as I untied him.

"You're a genius!" beamed Doug when he was free.

"Do you want to know the best part?" I asked.

"What?"

"Even with luring wolves and giving them a treat, I've still got enough of my original marinated meat to make sure that everyone at the barbecue enjoys the very best meat."

"You're amazing!" smiled Doug.

Day 30

It was the day of the barbecue and everywhere I looked, people were munching away on the meat I'd recovered from the adventurers. By the looks on their faces, they were savoring every mouthful.

"Well done," said Troy, coming over to pat me on the back. "You've really outdone yourself, Brutus. That first batch of meat you delivered was disgusting but this new lot is absolutely delicious. The barbecue is a total success and that's partly due to you. Although, of course, it's mainly due to my excellent organization skills. Without me, there wouldn't even be a barbecue for you to serve meat at."

"Of course," I nodded, restraining myself from the urge to roll my eyes.

"And there's no sign of that attack you were going on about," he went on. "I told you that there was nobody waiting to attack us. Maybe in the future you'll listen to me."

He moved away, going to talk to one of the visiting village leaders.

"He's really dumb!" said Doug who was by my side. "You were the one who made sure there was even a barbecue in the first place. If it wasn't for you and your incredible plan, the village would be overrun by adventurers right this second."

"I know, but when it comes to Troy, sometimes you've just got to let him think what he likes. Life is easier that way. Anyway, speaking of plans, I've got one that I think you're going to like."

"Really? What?"

"I've been speaking to your mom and dad…"

"Oh yeah." Doug's face fell. "I got into so much trouble from them for running away. They wouldn't believe me when I said I'd been kidnapped."

"Well, like I said, I've been speaking to them and they've agreed to let you stay with me when they go back home."

"Are you serious?" Doug practically squealed with excitement.

"Absolutely! I need an apprentice to help me in the butcher shop and since our family recipe can only be shared with family, who better than you to come and be my assistant?"

"Thank you! Oh, thank you!"

Doug threw his arms around me and squeezed me in a tight hug. I had a feeling that there was still more mischief to come from this little lad, but we'd also had a lot of fun together and I could do with an extra pair of hands about the place.

Besides, there was a possibility that the zombies hadn't taken out all of the adventurers. If they ever came back, I wanted at least one person by my side who knew about the thwarted invasion.

"Right, you. Let's get back to the barbecue. That meat isn't going to eat itself!"

As Doug skipped off to help himself to more food, I couldn't help but smile. Life was certainly more fun with him around.

71740701R00046

Made in the USA
Columbia, SC
03 June 2017